ENTREDISCIPLESHIP

A 31 Day Devotional for Biblical Entrepreneurship

Ronald Ainsley Callender Jr.

All scriptures unless otherwise noted are taken from the King James Version of the Bible

Please contact *info@ainsleyandtroupe.com* for inquiries.

ISBN - (Paperback) 978-1-7354356-3-3
ISBN - (ePub) 978-1-7354356-5-7
ISBN - (Audiobook) 978-1-7354356-8-8

CONTENTS

PROLOGUE

It is my great hope that you will understand and receive this work not only as an entrepreneur, but as a Christian. My spiritual lens for writing it was the truth of Jesus Christ, and I hope you will read it that way. Join me on this path as a Christ following, Holy Spirit filled entrepreneur. As children of God, my hope is that we are constantly given new levels of understanding and deeper wisdom to fully grasp this content through an awareness and relationship with Jesus Christ (2 Cor 5:17; Ez 36:26).

If you have never received Jesus Christ as your Lord and Savior, it is my even greater hope and prayer that you will take the leap of faith in this very moment to receive His salvation and that you would become a child of God. Romans 10:9-10 says,

> 9 That if thou shalt confess with thy mouth the Lord Jesus, and shalt believe in thine heart that God hath raised him from the dead, thou shalt be saved.
> 10 For with the heart man believeth unto righteousness; and with the mouth confession is made unto salvation.

Pray the following prayer aloud and believe it in your heart:

> Dear Lord Jesus Christ, please forgive me of my sins. I repent of my sins. I believe you died on the cross and rose from the grave for the remission of my sins. I invite you into my heart as my personal Lord and Savior. Thank you for saving me. In Jesus' name I pray. Amen.

By praying this prayer, if you truly believed it, you have now taken the first step as a child of God, having made Him the Lord and Savior of your life. I pray that He helps you understand both sides of this book, the natural and the spiritual, and that He begins to unlock brand new levels of understanding.

FOREWORD

When Ron told me he planned to write a book, my first thought was, "finally." Over the years, I've had the privilege of burning hours of time discussing various topics with Ron: everything from business, to faith, to relationships, to politics. Every time we converse, I always walk away with a more balanced and informed perspective, although the way that I reach those 'aha' moments is not entirely intuitive.

Whenever I want to corroborate my thoughts about a topic, I run them by Ron to get his input. Like clockwork, Ron always starts by listening intently. Once I am done exhausting my ideas, he normally just follows up by asking additional questions. Ron only gives his input if it adds color or value to our conversation. This may seem like an ineffective way to respond to someone, but I would argue that it is actually the most efficient and impactful way to give feedback. Ron is naturally an observant, poised, and patient person which consequently allows him to be such a great listener. He is able to sit back, collect all of the facts, and offer his thoughts in a comprehensive way.

With the help of Ron's feedback, I've been able to view my ideas more objectively regardless of how ridiculous, edgy, logical, or polished they may sound. Overall, I've benefited greatly from Ron's input and, as an added bonus, I've always had an outlet to share my ideas with someone that I trust.

Fortunately, Ron and I have had the opportunity to collaborate on numerous projects. One of my favorite collaborations happened back in 2015 when I was building Tailored for a King (TFAK), an online periodical that highlighted extraordinary black men living out their version of success. Ron had just started his first business, Ainsley & Troupe, and gained a lot of traction. After talking to him about his overall vision, I knew he would be an excellent person to feature on TFAK.

We created a script, plotted out the scenes, and got all of Ron's friends involved (something that Ron suggested immediately) after we realized that we needed some people sporting his A&T products.

The feature was meant to shine a light on Ron's approach to business, his definition of confidence, and his most powerful weapon, his relationship with Christ. While filming, I remember Ron remaining cool, calm, and collected no matter how many takes we did. The project was a huge success and garnered a lot of attention from our community of friends, family and fans.

While I genuinely appreciate our friendship and doing life together, I must admit our relationship didn't start that way. I first met Ron in 2012. I was introduced by our mutual friend, Kekura Musa. Kekura and I bonded (and still do) over our passion for technology, wealth building, business, and entrepreneurship. At the time we were both working on separate projects to get our feet wet in the business world. I remember being thoroughly impressed by Kekura's understanding of business.

One day during lunchtime, Kekura and I saw each other on campus of the University of Maryland, Baltimore County and decided to head towards the Commons building to get lunch. After catching up, we entered the Commons and noticed a group of guys hanging out near the bookstore; none of which I knew personally at the time. One of those guys happened to be Ron.

After noticing that I didn't know anyone, Kekura immediately introduced me to each of them, one by one. I felt elated and thankful for his gesture because at that moment my social life was in a rut to say the least.

When it came time to meet Ron, I briefly noticed he was standoffish. He didn't say much. It took a few more encounters on campus and seeing him visit my church before we officially warmed up to each other.

Looking back on it, I realize being reserved, calm, and discerning is just a part of Ron's nature. He is the type of person who believes in building trust over time. He has great relationships not by way of coincidence, but because he values people and is big on loyalty. As such, he is intentional about guarding his mind, emotions, and will so that it can best serve God and the people God has placed in his life.

This book is not only a testament to how far you can go with a strong foundation in Christ as a Christian, but also how much you can achieve with faith, diligence, submission, and passion as a businessperson.

My hope is that you will be blessed by Ron's words and feel his spirit in each lesson. He really has a heart for God and people. He is determined to live a purposeful life and invites you to do the same.

May God bless you and your community on your journey.

-- Carrington Dennis
(CEO, Carrington Creative Company)

Day 1

FIND YOUR PURPOSE

1 Peter 4:10 KJV. As every man hath received the gift, even so minister the same one to another, as good stewards of the manifold grace of God.

Finding our life's purpose is one of the most important tasks that we will have. Sadly, many people, without even realizing it, spend their entire lives searching—climbing to the tops of mountains, achieving goals, longing for significance—without ever finding their purpose. If we don't know what our purpose is, we won't know where to focus, and we will miss out on fulfillment, failing to give meaning to each day.

As 1 Peter 4:10 suggests, God has given each of us natural gifts and talents. Others may wish they had what comes naturally to you. Maybe you have excellent interpersonal skills, athletic or artistic ability, or musical talent. The list goes on and on, but it is our duty to find our gifts and talents and use them to serve one another with the grace that God demonstrates to us, bringing people closer to Christ. Our gifts and our purpose are intertwined. As purpose-led entrepreneurs, we must find our God-given task by discovering the gifts God has given us. Then, we must hone these gifts, seeking ways we can help others, and in doing so, create a revenue stream to support our work. Our gifts are not given to us *for us*. They are mechanisms for us to help others. Like Jonah, we can often feel our purpose and calling tugging at us, regardless of how much we run from them. We must keep in mind that there are many people who will not receive help and will face hardship if we continue to ignore our purposes and callings (Jnh 1-3).

Proverbs 18:16 A man's gift maketh room for him, and bringeth him before great men.

In Proverbs 18:16, God shows us that it is our gifts that will help us make our way through life and bring us before great men. When we properly operate within our God-given purpose and gifts, it will lead us into higher places and afford us opportunities to monetize our gifts by helping others. Once that happens, we will never have to *work* another day for the rest of our lives, because we will be enjoying ourselves so much, doing what we were created to do.

Success follows service. The greatest servant in history was Jesus Christ. He perfected His service by giving His life for us. When we use our lives to serve others, we serve God (Day 31). Success will chase and follow us once we get lost in serving others according to God's will. According to the Oxford English Dictionary, service is defined as, "*The action of helping or doing work for someone.*" Whose life can we improve through our business idea? What work can we do for them? Service to many leads to greatness. The person who serves the most typically earns the most. It's often said that an entrepreneur's salary is a direct reflection of the size of the problem he or she solves, and the number of people that he or she serves. Aim to bring great value and significance to your service.

Parallel Scriptures:

Romans 12:6-8; 2 Corinthians 4:15

Dear Lord,

Thank You for creating me in Your image. I thank You that You have already assigned my purpose in eternity. Lord, whatever purpose You have ordained for me to serve You, Your children, and the world You've created, make it plain to me. Give me the courage and the confidence to walk in the purpose You have for me, and to use the gifts You have given me to lead others to You. In Jesus' name I pray. Amen.

What is God saying to me? ________________________________

Day 2

YOU'RE ALREADY EQUIPPED FOR SUCCESS/FEELINGS OF INADEQUACY

Exodus 3:11 KJV. And Moses said unto God, Who am I, that I should go unto Pharaoh, and that I should bring forth the children of Israel out of Egypt?

Immediately after the world fell into sin in the Garden of Eden, God stepped in with a plan to save the world that would one day culminate in the resurrection of Jesus Christ. God's redemptive plan went into a new stage when He called a man named Abraham (Abram at first) from whom He would create a nation to bless the entire world. God warned Abraham that this nation would spend over four hundred years enslaved in Egypt, but that at just the right time, God would step in again to set them free and bring them back to the land of promise. The task of freeing Abraham's descendants, the Israelites, fell to a man named Moses.

Moses' task was one of the most important in the Old Testament, but Moses felt incredibly inadequate for the job. He came up with numerous excuses for why God got it wrong and why he was not the guy for the task. But to Moses' chagrin, God had a ready answer for every one of Moses' objections. Moses made excuses, and God asked, "What's that in your hand?" In that exact moment, Moses was holding his shepherd's staff. "Throw it down," God said. Moses obeyed, and the staff transformed into a serpent as it hit the ground! God explained that this was only one of the signs and wonders that Moses would be empowered to do in front of Pharaoh and the Egyptians.

At the beginning of our entrepreneurial journeys, it may appear that we possess very little. But if we will have faith, we will know that God can use our very little to do very much. He can accomplish whatever mighty works He wants to accomplish through us if we will just be faithful. *Imposter syndrome* is a natural and common feeling among entrepreneurs. But the truth is, the more inadequate we feel, the greater God will use us in our obedience, because the less we feel adequate in ourselves, the more we will trust in God and not in our own abilities. In this way, God will get the most glory in the end.

Take this example: Moses had a problem with his speech. One may logically assume that in order to lead a large number of people like Moses did, one would have to be a great orator and an extremely charismatic leader. However, Moses had been living as a simple shepherd for forty years since fleeing for his life from his boyhood home in Egypt. Moses did not realize that it was his skills as a shepherd that God wanted to use. Moses had led sheep through the wilderness; now he would lead the sheep of God's pasture, the

Israelites. In this way, God would accomplish through Moses a great and mighty deliverance. Moses felt inadequate, but it was God who accomplished His purposes through the inadequate man whom God called.

Parallel Scriptures:

Phil 4:13; Romans 8:31

Dear Lord,

I thank You for placing a specific calling on my life and a purpose according to Your perfect plan. Help me overcome my unbelief so that I can understand that I have everything I need at my disposal right now to start my journey. I am complete. I lack nothing. Whatever I need to get started, is already here with me. I know that You will supply whatever else is needed at just the right time, because You are a generous God who will not call me to do anything that You will not equip me to do. You will not withhold any good thing from me. Thank You in advance for multiplying and growing the gifts and abilities I am starting with. In Jesus' name I pray. Amen.

What is God saying to me? ________________________________

Day 3

DON'T LOOK BACK

Luke 9:62 KJV. And Jesus said unto him, "No man, having put his hand to the plough, and looking back, is fit for the kingdom of God."

The time for Jesus Christ to return to heaven was approaching. Jesus and His disciples had turned their focus to Jerusalem where His earthly ministry would come to a brutal, painful, but victorious end. As Jesus traveled along the roads with His disciples, He encountered several men who stated their intentions to follow Him. One of them said, "I will follow thee; but let me first go bid them farewell, which are at home at my house" (Lk 9:61). To this, Jesus replied, "No man having put his hand to the plough [plow], and looking back, is fit for the kingdom of God." (62).

Putting your hand to a plow was an expression that meant *taking up a new task.* It means the same thing today. In this passage of Scripture, Jesus was referring to the task of beginning a Spiritual walk with Him. In the agricultural society in which Jesus lived, His audience would've known exactly what that expression meant. When operating a plow, a plowman must focus on the path ahead in order to keep a straight line forward in the earth. This would allow the plowman to reap a full and productive harvest. However, if the plowman looks behind him, he risks cutting a crooked line in front of him, jeopardizing his harvest.

Spiritually, if we look back at the things we left behind to follow Christ, we jeopardize our future walk with Christ, and ultimately, our fitness for the kingdom of God. Jesus takes this point so seriously that He advised the man not to turn back to say goodbye to his family. Our entrepreneurial journeys can be looked at in a similar way. If we begin to look back at the things we've already overcome during our journeys (relationships that hindered us, bad habits, etc.), we risk falling back into the same unproductive things, jeopardizing our business and the progress we have made. Don't look back, but set your face forward, eyes on the path ahead for a full and productive harvest spiritually and in business.

Parallel Scriptures:

Revelation 3:15, Matthew 12:30

Dear Lord,

Thank You for delivering me from the things in my life that do not benefit me in my walk with You. Thank You for removing those things that would get in the way of my business. Lord, please continue to prune my life of anything that would jeopardize my chances of producing a harvest, both in my spiritual life, and in my business. Lord, give me the confidence, peace and wherewithal to keep my focus forward without looking back on the things which I have left behind. I decree and declare that You will fill any voids in me with only blessings that will maximize my harvests. In Jesus' name I pray. Amen.

What is God saying to me?

Day 4

ANXIETY & PATIENCE

Phil 4:6-7 KJV. 6 Be careful for nothing; but in everything by prayer and supplication with thanksgiving let your requests be made known unto God. 7 And the peace of God, which passeth all understanding, shall keep your hearts and minds through Christ Jesus.

The Philippian church had much to be anxious about. There was poverty, persecution, and political uncertainty. From a Roman prison, Paul wrote them a letter in response to the many things they had been worried about. On top of everything else going on, there had been some wolves, false teachers who had come among them to pressure them to turn from grace and live according to the law that no one in history had been able to save themselves by. This led to great internal discord and disunity in the church.

Paul explained that much of their anxiety resulted from wanting something. He advised the Philippians not to be anxious or to worry about the current conditions, but to pray about them, always being thankful to God for what He has already done and is planning to do. In his advice, Paul does not promise them that God will automatically change their circumstances. However, as verse 7 indicates, God does promise to bestow on them a peace that surpasses all understanding. Although God is more than able to change things in an instant, He does not promise to do so. But God does promise that He will always be with us and grant us the peace to endure the trials from which, according to His purposes for us, He does not always deliver us.

Although Paul's audience in this letter was the Philippian church, the premise applies to us as believing entrepreneurs as well. Throughout our entrepreneurial journeys, we'll undoubtedly face moments of anxiety. We can picture the final vision, but we know the great multitude of work separating us from what we can see, causing angst and internal battles. Verse 6 instructs us to be careful for nothing. Many times, we are full of care [*careful*] - that is, we care too much. Numerous times throughout the Bible we are told not to be *careful* or *anxious* (1 Peter 5:7*; Psalms 55:22*). Why don't we heed Paul's message, and let God know all our goals and desires in business, as we thank Him for what He has already accomplished and still is going to accomplish through us. As aforementioned, God can give us exactly what we want right now, but *He will not limit Himself to that.* What's often more important is to have peace to continue the grind should God decide to delay giving us our desires, knowing we will continue to trust Him no matter His timing. What God does in us while we wait can be more significant than what we are waiting for. We should be direct with God about our business goals and plans, and anticipate His peace and the increase of our patience.

Parallel Scriptures:

1 Peter 5:7, Psalms 55:22

Dear Lord,

I thank You for everything You have already done for me and through me. I humbly make the following requests known to You:____

____

____

____

____

____

Lord, grant me Your peace that surpasses all understanding as I endure the tests of life and of entrepreneurship. Allow me to combat any anxiety in my heart with Your perfect love and perfect peace. In Jesus' name I pray. Amen.

What is God saying to me? ______________________________

Day 5

URGENCY VS. COMPLACENCY

Psalms 90:3-10 NIV. 3 You turn people back to dust, saying, "Return to dust, you mortals." 4 A thousand years in your sight are like a day that has just gone by, or like a watch in the night. 5 Yet you sweep people away in the sleep of death-they are like the new grass of the morning: 6 In the morning it springs up new, but by evening it is dry and withered. 10 Our days may come to seventy years, or eighty, if our strength endures; yet the best of them are but trouble and sorrow, for they quickly pass, and we fly away."

Scholars think that Psalm 90 was the only one written by Moses. As Moses prayed to God, he alluded several times to the brevity of human life.

Many people believe they have all the time in the world to accomplish their goals and missions, but this is exactly opposite of the truth. In verse 12, Moses prays, "Lord, teach us to number our days, that we may gain a heart of wisdom." This means that we should live each day as if it was our last, because we do not know what tomorrow may bring. Would we not spend our time with more focus and purpose if only we understood how short they are? God can take our life from us tomorrow.

In verse 6, man's life is likened to the lifespan of grass, represented by one day, comprised of one morning and one evening. The key ingredient is wisdom, and this is what Moses prayed for. If we are not going to spend our time foolishly and unplanned, then wisdom is what we need. If we understood that our days were numbered, we would not waste time. This is critical to entrepreneurs because we have exactly zero time to waste. However, there is a balance between hurry and stagnation, and finding it is crucial (Day 4). Every minute of every day must be calculated for the highest impact. We must spend time at the micro level to see that we meet our daily short-term goals while keeping an eye on the macro level and our long-term vision. This requires patience, diligence, and needs time for regular reflection for recalibrating (Day 30).

Why? So that each minute of each day is accounted for, and no time is wasted. We can always make back money that is lost. We cannot get back our lost time. Do not procrastinate. Spend time planning in order to make intelligent use of your time. Every minute, think, "What is the very best way to spend this minute in light of what I say my goals and vision are?" Not doing this is the very best way to fail to see progress.

Parallel Scripture:

James 4:14

Dear Lord,

I know that our time is short on this earth. I want to honor You and make the very most of all my time here on earth. Help me not to frivolously squander away any of it. Please place in front of me the things that are meant to help me to continue to walk in Your purpose for me for Your glory. Grant me the wisdom to see those time wasters that hold me up, and give me the confidence to adjust my life accordingly. In Jesus' name I pray. Amen.

What is God saying to me? ________________________________

Day 6

DO NOT TELL EVERYONE YOUR PLANS

Matthew 7:6 KJV. Give not that which is holy unto the dogs, neither cast ye your pearls before swine, lest they trample them under their feet, and turn again and rend you.

Do not tell everyone your ideas. Do not lend your strength and gifts to all people. Not everyone should be privy to your vision. We must be careful about who we share the good news of our business goals and successes with. Some will not be able to take us seriously. We must share our goals with only certain people who won't downplay, discredit, or dismiss them. Our plans should be shared carefully with those who won't feel threatened or displace their insecurities about their own ideas, gifts, goals, visions, and plans on us.

Jesus gave the command in Matthew 7:6 so that His followers could watch out for "dogs" and "swine," those people who would reject, ridicule, blaspheme, or underappreciate the Good News of His coming. Dogs and swine do not appreciate what is holy. They do not value pearls of any price, let alone pearls of great price. By the same token, there are those who will be unable to be supportive of your plans and your vision for your business. They will not want to see and appreciate your gifts and the value you bring to the marketplace. They will discourage you, put up obstacles, and cause you to question what you were so sure about. These people are not to be confused with those who are actually for you, but provide helpful and critical feedback. We need these types of people to develop the confidence to hear criticism. Be advised that there is a difference.

There will be many people who are ready to hear our message. We Christians are charged with spreading the Gospel of Jesus Christ, but we are not to force it on people, because in order to be accepted, it must be accepted freely. Also, we are not responsible for other people's response to the Gospel. When our message faces rejection, Jesus simply calls us to move on and go elsewhere. We are not to stop spreading the message altogether (Mt 10:14), but to keep looking for fertile soil.

It is important to note that this chapter of Scripture begins with *judgment.* We have not been called to be hypocritically judgmental (Mt 7:1-5), but we are called to have discernment in our dealings (Day 9). It takes a strong spirit of discernment to identify the "dogs" and "swine" in our lives. This should be done prayerfully. Jesus notoriously spent time with tax collectors, prostitutes, and other people that the Bible simply calls "sinners." These were people with a sinful past but who were responsive to His message. Meanwhile, there were the religious people of the day who felt threatened by Jesus' power, popularity, and lack of willingness to defer to *them.*

Whether you are spreading the Gospel or spreading the message of your business (in a godly way for the good of the world), learn who is truly responsive and who is a hindrance to you. Jesus never closed the door on someone who wanted to come to Him sincerely. He also never stopped moving forward, allowing no "dogs" or "swine" to sway Him from His mission.

Parallel Scriptures:

Matthew 10:14; 1 Corinthians 2:15-16; Luke 8:53-54

Dear Lord,

You have given me a message to spread to the world around me. Thank You for that. Please grant me wisdom to discern where the most fertile ground is for the planting of the seeds you have placed in my hands. Give me all the strength I need to continue to spread the messages you have entrusted to me without any discouragement if they are met with opposition. I trust in You for the fertile soil and for the good outcomes that You have prepared for me. In Jesus' name I pray. Amen.

What is God saying to me?

Day 7

FIND YOUR NICHE AND CONQUER THAT FIRST

James 1:8 KJV. A double minded man is unstable in all his ways.

Find your niche and stick to it. Don't fish around trying to solve tons of other problems. If you try to satisfy everyone, you'll end up satisfying no one.

Addressing the believers among the twelve tribes of Israel that were scattered among the nations, James poses in this passage that we should ask God for whatever it is that we lack, because God is a generous giver. However, once we ask, we should not doubt. The person who doubts is like a wave of the ocean and is forever tossed to and fro. James calls this kind of person "double minded" and "unstable in all he does."

In business, we must set our minds on what we have started out to do and not doubt the outcome. To take this further, it even benefits us to set out to conquer one niche area or problem at a time, sticking with it until it is accomplished. What is your big idea? What areas of your business are you most interested in? What door have you seen open for you that you already have a foot in? Continue walking through that door and don't stop until you have accomplished your goal.

If your goal is to make toys for toddlers, stick to that niche. Do not begin branching out until you have first reached your goal. Don't get distracted making toys for adults, or some other product in a totally different market, until you have gained your momentum in the toddler toy market. Sometimes we stray away from the goal because we get bored. Other times it happens because we are afraid we will miss some other opportunity, and that we have chosen the wrong niche. Sometimes we get caught up trying to be all things to all people, seeking to solve many problems in many niches at once, failing in all of them, and satisfying no one sufficiently to succeed.

When pursuing our goals, we must go all in with each task. We must be willing to sacrifice time and money, allocating them towards our most important goals. God doesn't bless us when we are wishy washy with Him or the things we set out to do (Rev 3:15; Mt 6:24) (Day 3). We should remember this along our journey and focus on one task at a time.

Parallel Scriptures:

Revelation 3:15; Matthew 6:24

Dear Lord,

I thank You for the creative mind that You have blessed me with and the many ideas that You have put there. Show me, Lord, how to prioritize those ideas, and help me to understand which tasks should take priority. I don't want to be double-minded. Make me a person of focus, that I could carry every task through to the end for the good of the world and for Your glory. I know that there are specific things that You have created me for. Guide me to those things and make me know them when I see them. In Jesus' name I pray. Amen.

What is God saying to me?

Day 8

THE LITTLE THINGS

Matthew 25:23 KJV. His lord said unto him, Well done, good and faithful servant; thou hast been faithful over a few things, I will make thee ruler over many things: enter thou into the joy of thy lord.

In Matthew 25:14-28, Jesus told his disciples the Parable of the Talents. He said that the Kingdom of God was like a man traveling to a far country who had given his money to three of his servants. He told them each to invest their money until he came back to see what kind of return they could make on it for him. Each of the servants was given a different amount of money according to his ability. The first man received five talents (bags of gold); the second received two; the last servant received only one.

When the master returned for an account from his servants, he found out that the servant with five talents had invested wisely, producing five more. When he settled with the second servant who had received the two talents, he found that he had produced two more. Both men were rewarded with praise and were given even greater responsibility for the next time.

But when the master approached the man with one talent, he was not pleased. Afraid he would lose his one bag of gold, the unfaithful servant hid his investment in the ground, though he was aware that it was in his master's nature and character to invest and reap. He was afraid and did nothing. The master was unhappy and punished him severely. He had not expected five talents in return, or even two, but he was expecting *something*. Even if the servant had lost his talent by faithfully investing, but failing, he would have been commended for trying. But to not try was considered faithlessness.

God has created each of us with specific gifts, talents, and opportunities. He expects us to use these to serve one another and build His kingdom (Day 1). God has so ordered the universe that when we are faithful over the smallest things, those things will lead to bigger things. In your business, it might be faithfully returning emails on time, or faithfully knocking on doors, or taking care of the people who work for you. It is giving your best every time, and at every task in front of you. What is the condition of your financial statements? Have you kept them carefully? How well organized is your inventory? Is it in shambles, or is it in order? Are you ready for an audit, or to consider a prospective partner?

Think about it. Would you give an employee $1,000 to deposit in the bank if last week that employee lost a $10 check? I hope you would not. God is the same way. When God sees that we are faithful with what He has given us to do, He will add increase. Because of this amazing principle, it matters very little what you start out with, but it matters a great deal what you do with it (Day 31).

Dear Lord,

I thank You for everything You have given me in my business, from the smallest to the largest resources and opportunities. I confess that I have had nothing that was not generously supplied by You, the Giver of all good gifts. Help me to be a steward of the small things in the same way as I do the large things. Help me to be diligent in looking after every single aspect of my business, regardless of size, scope, or relative importance. I know that there is not a single thing that You have given me that You don't find important. Help me to see what You see, and do what You would have me to do. In Jesus' name I pray. Amen.

What is God saying to me?

Day 9

GODLY DISCERNMENT

1 John 4:1 KJV. Beloved, believe not every spirit, but try the spirits whether they are of God: because many false prophets are gone out into the world.

John's admonition to "try the spirits" was about discerning between what spiritual influences were from God, and good, and those that were demonic, and bad. This is critical for every believer because it is important for all God's people to be discerning, loving right, and shunning wrong. We must be wise (Mt 10:16). We must know the truth and test all information according to what we know from Scripture and wisdom.

In the same fashion, we must learn to test any information we are given according to what we know of the sources of that information and the motives of the ones giving it. The Bible says that, "He that walketh with wise men shall be wise: but a companion of fools shall be destroyed" (Pr 13:20). It also says, "Go from the presence of a foolish man, when thou perceivest not in him the lips of knowledge" (Pr

14:7). According to these verses, we should not only ignore the speech of fools, but we should avoid associating with them all together. When we do have to hear them, we must know how to filter out foolishness.

God (through John) cautions us not to believe every spirit or person claiming to come in the name of God. He says that we can discern their origin by whether we hear them deny or confirm that Jesus Christ has come in the flesh (1 Jn 4:2-3).

In business, we must be cautious concerning who we seek counsel from, discerning intentions every step of the way. There are a few reasons for this. First, the motives of our advisors could be less than pure. We must learn what questions to ask to flesh out those motives. Do they want to take our business? Are they insecure and would feel better about themselves if we failed? Do they have a hidden agenda to gain power over us, to use us for their own purposes? How genuine do they seem? Most will show signs when they switch from a normal conversation to using instrumental language, maneuvering us to the place they want us. Are they flattering? Do they suddenly seem nervous? That may be a sign of an agenda.

There are others whose motives are pure, but they do not quite understand what you are doing, so their advice is less helpful. Watch out for those with a very limited scope of knowledge. They will see everything from their tiny lenses. Learn to sense in your spirit when the information is not quite right, or the motive is not quite pure. Pray, fast, and learn the Scriptures to become a more discerning and aware person. Always hone your vision (Day 11) so that you remember in each conversation not only *what* you are doing, but *why*. With all that said, remain teachable, and love truth. Occasionally, we find ourselves in the unfortunate position of realizing we've been wrong about something. When an advisor is giving us good advice, but we just don't like it so we are pushing back anxiously, that may be a sign that we need to listen. Don't lie to yourself. You'll regret it later.

Parallel Scripture:

1 Corinthians 2:15

Dear Lord,

Thank You that You have created an objective reality where there is right and there is wrong. All reality is in You. Help me to see what is in the people around me, that I would be gentle as a dove, but as wise as a serpent. Give me a powerful spirit of discernment and strengthen it every day. Open my eyes to see the truth behind all the motives and intentions of every person I encounter. Give me the moral courage to address each person accordingly and justly. Help me to say what needs to be said in love and mercy. In Jesus' name I pray. Amen.

What is God saying to me? ______________________

Day 10

SPEAK SUCCESS

Proverbs 18:21 KJV. Death and life are in the power of the tongue: and they that love it shall eat the fruit thereof.

The power of words is highly underappreciated, but the words we speak are extremely important. In this passage of Scripture, God is instructing us on this point. Words have the power to bring life into things, and they have the power to take life out of things. The kind of words we use will dictate the nature of the fruit which grows. Our words are the seeds sown by us, and the fruit will come one way or another.

As it always eventually does, science has proven that the Bible is true on this point. The effects of positive speech have proven remarkable in multiple fields like medicine, business, counseling, and more. Speaking out with the conscious mind is a wonderful and sure way of training the unconscious mind concerning what is true. The unconscious mind controls our emotions, and probably even our physical health. The conscious mind controls our unconscious mind *if we are deliberate about training it.* Speaking out God's truth is one sure way to do that.

God has put power on the tongue to bless others and to bring things into reality. Praying out loud is powerful because it tells not only God what you want, but also yourself and the rest of heaven. We ourselves are "transformed by the renewing of [our] minds" (Ro 12:2). Others will be affected by how we bless them with our words as well. Additionally, agreeing with others with words in prayer is a powerful way to make things happen (Mt 18:19). Surround yourself with positive and encouraging people who will pray with you and speak life and blessings to you.

It should also be stated that the opposite is true as well. As much power as the tongue has been given to bless and transform for good, it can also be used against us as a weapon for cursing and death. Take great care in what you say. It is no fun to have a negative and destructive thought, but we make it much more powerful when we choose to speak it out. We curse others when we fail to guard our speech around them. Understand this great power and take control of your tongue. If you will mind the words that come from your mouth, you will plant seeds that will eventually grow into the fruit of success and godliness.

Parallel Scriptures:

Romans 4:17; Mark 11:22-24; Proverbs 12:18; Matthew 12:36; Matthew 17:20

Dear Lord,

You are the Word. Your Son was the Word made flesh. I know that words have great power. Thank You that You created me in Your own image with the power to create and destroy, especially the power in my tongue. Help me to know the great responsibility that I bear with this gift, and help me to guard my tongue so that I am not careless or frivolous with my words. Thank You for putting power in the words that I speak. Give me the right words at the right time and the love and courage to speak them in a way that makes good things happen. In Jesus' name I pray. Amen.

What is God saying to me? ____________________

Day 11

HAVE A VISION

Proverbs 29:18 KJV. Where there is no vision, the people perish: but he that keepeth the law, happy is he.

This verse can be read two ways, and both are true. Without "prophetic" vision, as some translations put it, there can be no true understanding of the truth of Scripture, and one cannot "keepeth the law," and so be "happy." But a more common understanding is that someone must hold to a vision of the future as a guide for going forward. For the Christian, it is good to keep a vision of heaven, of Christ, and of the goal of the reward on the great day of judgement. By doing so, our decision making is simpler, our paths are well lit, our future is certain.

Our businesses are the same. It is pertinent to know, or at least have an idea of the destination for our business efforts (Day 12). Without a vision, our business will aimlessly go through the motions. There will be activity, effort, and energy expended, but opportunities will be missed and complacency will settle in. Aiming at nothing will reach the goal of nothingness every time.

Without a measurable, specific vision, we cannot track our progress. We cannot know the position and status of our company. When we have a vision and stick to the process of completing that vision, we reduce the amount of confusion and hopelessness we experience. A business without an endgame is going nowhere. We will do extra work, and we will duplicate efforts when we fail to have a vision. Business is too competitive, and the environment is too hard for us to take off without a destination in mind and a map to get there. Become intentional. What do you want your end result to be? Don't start a course of action until you can see the end result first.

Dear Lord,

Thank You for the vision You have given me for my business ventures. I ask You to mold the vision according to Your great purposes for me. Lord, let me not forget the vision You have written on my heart, and help me to keep the vision on the forefront of my mind as I make decisions every day, and as I decide what to do with each moment You have blessed me with. I confess that sometimes I find myself going through the motions because I forget this very important reality. Lord, grant me the grace to remember that without vision, people perish. In Jesus' name I pray. Amen.

What is God saying to me? ____________________

Day 12

WRITE YOUR VISION DOWN

Habakkuk 2:2 KJV. And the Lord answered me, and said, Write the vision, and make it plain upon tables, that he may run that readeth it.

In this verse, God tells the prophet Habakkuk to write the vision or revelation on large tablets that were likely made of boxwood and carved with an iron pen. This was often a way of getting a message to the public, which would then make it around to the whole nation by runners. The carving would be hung up at the prophet's own house or at the temple. It would be legible and plain, that others could understand and obey, telling everyone possible.

This is good advice for those of us who are entrepreneurs. We should write down our vision in plain, legible language in a place that we will regularly see. Instead of writing on tablets, as Habakkuk was instructed to do, we should create vision boards and business plans. We should pray over these vision boards and business plans that they would be a product of what we have received from God, keep us following His plans and accomplishing His purposes, and that God would guide our steps using them (Day 29). They should be succinct and written in plain language so that any lay person could understand what you've written.

Writing down our vision is powerful and extremely important because it will guide us throughout our entrepreneurial journey. It will provide us with purpose, goals, and daily direction (Day 11). There is always potential that we will need to present our vision and business plan to investors and banks, so ensuring that they contain plain language and convey the good news we intend to communicate is critical.

Consider that God took the time through thousands of years, using over forty authors, and by the power of His Holy Spirit to write down His own vision and plan for saving the world. Consider that it was His own instructions to the prophet. Writing down our vision and plan will go a long way towards their accomplishment.

Parallel Scripture:

Daniel 12:4

Dear Lord,

Thank You, Father, that You saw fit to bless me with a vision for business. I confess, Lord, that I could not have come up with it on my own. I give You my mind and my heart so that You can mold them as You please, and put whatever You want in them. I pray that You will help me to break the vision You have given me down into parts and to articulate every aspect of the vision as clearly and as detailed as possible in writing. I ask that You bless this written statement with Your power and with Your favor, so that anyone who may read it will be inspired by it for Your glory. In Jesus' name I pray. Amen.

What is God saying to me?

Day 13

YOUR VISION AND YOUR WORK ETHIC

James 2:14-26 KJV. 26 For as the body without the spirit is dead, so faith without works is dead also.

We can have the most powerful and well-articulated vision in the world, but if our work ethic does not match the size of the dream, it is a dead mission. God promises us that He blesses us and adds no sorrow (Pr 10:22). He will not bless our business with a million orders to fill if He knows we cannot handle them because our work ethic is not strong enough. That would bring misery to our life and undermine the original blessing. It would bring much sorrow.

James tells us that if we don't have *works*, then there is no evidence that our faith is alive. True faith will spur on action. In the same way that it is not enough to have faith with no works as Christians, faith in our entrepreneurial vision will be useless without the accompanying works. We can have the greatest possible faith in our vision, but we must have the work ethic to go with it, or our vision will die.

Abraham's willingness to sacrifice his son, Isaac, is what perfected his faith. Isaac was a miracle child born to a barren and elderly mother, Sara. Abraham backed up his faith in God's promises when he obeyed God and offered up Isaac as a sacrifice. God had tested the genuineness of his faith and, of course, presented a ram in place of Isaac (much like He would present His own Son, Jesus, in our place) to be sacrificed. When we back up our faith with our works, it justifies the level of faith that we have, showing God that we are serious, and that we are putting our money where our mouth is. As God did with Abraham and the ram in the thicket, God will intervene divinely for us when He sees our faith matched by our work.

Due to the original sin of man, our labor here on Earth became toilsome forever (Gen 3:17-19). Our flesh will major in excuses to skip out on doing the work necessary to make the vision a reality. Do whatever you must to keep your vision in a place in your mind and heart that will motivate you to action, because "faith without works is dead."

Dear Lord,

Thank You for the faith You have given me to begin this endeavor. I know also that, just like any worthy endeavor, it will take hard work to accomplish. I pray that You show me what exact work is necessary to make progress in this venture, and that You would grant me the courage and the strength to work at it diligently. I pray that I may complete the assignment that You in Your sovereign will have given me, and that I would have a supernatural ability to do more than I thought I was capable of doing. Glorify Yourself in this, and accomplish Your will through the hard work I do by Your powerful Spirit in me. In Jesus' name I pray. Amen.

What is God saying to me? ______________________________

Day 14

STUDY YOUR CRAFT AND LOVE THE WORK

Psalm 119:15-16 NLT. 15 I will study your commandments and reflect on your ways. 16 I will delight in your decrees and not forget your word.

God desires that we know Him intimately. He is not some distant God or some concept in oblivion, but our Father who wants a relationship with us. As such, He has given us an incredible amount of revelation in order to study Him and to know His ways, that we could not only delight in His ways, but in God Himself.

The same way God calls us to study, know, and apply His Word, we should be diligent to study, know, and apply ourselves to our respective businesses and industries. Hard work is just that, *hard*. However, it is made enjoyable when we learn to delight in the work. The greater our skill and craftsmanship, the more we will delight in it. Don't despair that it takes some time and effort to become great at what you do. Learn to love the process of growing, just as you love the process of getting to know your Father in heaven.

If you are doing what you are passionate about and called to do, then you can weather the hard seasons (Day 17). We have to be lifetime students of God's Word, *and* of the tools of our craft, always looking to expand our knowledge of both. With the advent of the internet, information is more available than ever before and at every moment. One of the easiest things to do now is find the information to research our craft and our business industry. This requires almost no money, and doesn't even require interaction with others.

Too many people short circuit this part of the process, loving the idea of success, but are unwilling to put in the hours to achieve mastery. If it is worth doing, it is worth doing skillfully. For the glory of God, learn your craft as you learn your God. Success and blessings will follow you wherever you go.

Parallel Scriptures:

2 Timothy 2:15; Psalms 1:1-3

Dear Lord,

I praise You for every aspect of the endeavor that You have assigned me, both the easy parts *and* the hard parts. I pray that You would give me the understanding to delight in learning every part of my craft. Steer me in the direction towards the greatest and most beneficial sources of the knowledge I require to fulfill the purposes You have for me. Fill me with Your Spirit for the energy and curiosity to uncover the truths set before me. Help me to use them to accomplish the purposes You have for me. In Jesus' name I pray. Amen.

What is God saying to me?

Day 15

NOTHING NEW UNDER THE SUN

Ecclesiastes 1:9-10 KJV. 9 The thing that hath been, it is that which shall be; and that which is done is that which shall be done: and there is no new thing under the sun. 10 Is there any thing whereof it may be said, See, this is new? it hath been already of old time, which was before us.

Solomon implores us to learn early in our lives what he discovered later in his: There is nothing new under the sun. Although methods may change, and mediums may change, and always have throughout history, especially in the last two hundred years, the root principles do not change. For example, we might be tempted to think that the internet and social media has changed communication. However, the *concept* of communication has not changed. The methods and the speed in which we communicate are what has changed through innovations in technology.

Or consider land travel. Travel has been around since the first man was created with his two functioning legs. Perhaps, very quickly he realized that he could hop on the back of a four-legged creature and go further. Eventually, the wheel came along and made carrying cargo much easier. And after a really long time, the first primitive cars, trains and planes arrived. And don't forget about roads, and interstate highway systems. Now? It boggles the mind not only how fast we can travel from one place to another, but what kind of comfort we can experience in the process.

The problems we will face as entrepreneurs are not new. Additionally, it is likely that our business idea is not totally new. Many of us will adopt the same purpose in life, with the same business goals. We will be competitors. At that point it is all about execution. He who best executes an idea wins. By researching and practicing our craft (Day 14), seeking a mentor for advice, and benchmarking companies with similar ideas, we can learn from those who have already faced most of our obstacles. We must learn from those who have already traveled the road before us and take notes. We must even stand on their strong shoulders, and establish our journey, remembering there is nothing new under the sun.

Dear Lord,

Thank You for the men and women who You have called before me and for their good examples of similar work. Help me to be humble and teachable. Help me to be open to the solutions they present to the same problems I have which they have already solved. If I am meant to have a mentor, please sovereignly place that person in my life at just the right time, and show me, so that

they can impart lessons to me that will ultimately lead to my success and Your glory. In Jesus' name I pray. Amen.

What is God saying to me? ______________________________

Day 16

PEOPLE MAY CALL YOU CRAZY

Genesis 6:8 KJV. But Noah found grace in the eyes of the Lord.

In Genesis 6-9 the Bible tells the story of Noah. In the days of Noah, there was much sin and evil in the world. God had made man in His image, and had given him the power to make choices between good and evil. Amazingly, man had chosen evil. In Genesis 6:5 it says, "And God saw that the wickedness of man was great in the earth, and that every imagination of the thoughts of his heart was only evil continually." God brought a judgment on the earth and sent a flood to wipe out every living thing and restart mankind with Noah's family. As a result of the whole revelation of God available to us today, we can see that this was only one step in an entire redemptive process that began in the Garden of Eden with the promise that Eve's offspring would crush the head of the serpent (Gen 3:15). This would then culminate in the return of Jesus Christ who was killed for our sins and raised to life, that those who believe in Him would have eternal life (Jn 3:16).

God instructed Noah to build the ark that would shelter his family along with at least a pair of every kind of living land and air creature, so that they too could repopulate the earth. While the Bible does not mention explicitly how long it took Noah to build the ark, Bible scholars generally agree that it would have taken between fifty and seventy years to complete. And while the Bible also does not tell us explicitly that those around Noah called him foolish for building the ark, it has been a common assumption that they did. Can you imagine what people would think if you built a boat of that size, nowhere near the sea, in a place that did not receive much rain? And remember, the flood started seven days after the boat was constructed. Imagine if people saw you and your family inside the boat on dry land with two of every land and air creature for seven days. It is safe to assume Noah may have been ridiculed mercilessly.

On our own journeys we must learn to put our heads down, as Noah did, and work on the calling and tasks God has given us. Others may see you pursuing your vision and call you crazy as you go along your way. We will not be able to get everyone on board with our vision. The example we are setting with our hard work and discipline may be the only time they begin to believe in you. For those who call us crazy, let's not tell them what will happen, let's show them. Our ideas are only crazy until they come to pass.

Parallel Scripture:

Mark 5:35-43

Dear Lord,

Thank You for allowing me to hear Your calling loud and clear. Help me to remain steadfast in the face of criticism or the ill opinions of other people. Help me to remember that I don't work for the praise of man, but for the glory of You and for the good of the world. I pray that my completed projects, products, and processes would all be a testimony of You and Your faithfulness to all those who see Your work in my life. Help me to have patience and grace for those who are not able to be supportive for whatever reason. In Jesus' name I pray. Amen.

What is God saying to me?

Day 17

WEATHER THE SEASONS/BIRTH PAINS

Ecclesiastes 3:1-8 KJV. 1 To every thing there is a season, and a time to every purpose under the heaven: 2 A time to be born, and a time to die; a time to plant, and a time to pluck up that which is planted; 3 A time to kill, and a time to heal; a time to break down, and a time to build up; 4 A time to weep, and a time to laugh; a time to mourn, and a time to dance; 5 A time to cast away stones, and a time to gather stones together; a time to embrace, and a time to refrain from embracing; 6 A time to get, and a time to lose; a time to keep, and a time to cast away; 7 A time to rend, and a time to sew; a time to keep silence, and a time to speak; 8 A time to love, and a time to hate; a time of war, and a time of peace.

It would be really nice if our entrepreneurial journeys followed a straight line forever upward. Unfortunately, that is not how it works. Our businesses will have seasons of ups and downs, profits and losses, busy seasons and slow seasons. There is a time for all of it. We must learn to identify the storms and become strong and stable enough to weather them. Perhaps we need to pivot, but we do not need to quit.

Successfully weathering the tough seasons in business is what makes the difference between strong companies and weak ones that eventually fail. If our ventures are going to stand the test of time, then we must plan for this eventuality. How much debt do you have in your business? How much cash do you have to weather the losses and unforeseen circumstances in the business climate (like an economic recession or pandemic)? Build this stability into your business plan and you will build longevity.

Some of the strongest storms we will face will turn out to be birth pains. Have you ever known a woman who was having a baby? The baby grows and grows for nine months. There is more and more discomfort until, at last, it is time for the birth, and also time for the greatest storm, labor! This last stage is the most painful, but brings forth the most joy. The last stretch of a hard business cycle can be the same way and birth some new levels of success, as crucial elements of our ventures are brought into the world (Mt 24:8 NIV).

Parallel Scripture:

Luke 21:9

Dear Lord,

I know that You are in control of the universe and do all things in it for Your glory and our good. I know and am thankful that even hard seasons have great purpose. Thank You for each and every season that has come and will come in my entrepreneurial

and faith journeys. Grant me the great wherewithal to weather every season along the way. Help me, Lord, to understand and learn each lesson in each stage and season You take me through. Be glorified in the steadfastness that You work in me. In Jesus' name I pray. Amen.

What is God saying to me? ______________________________

Day 18

SYNERGY & THE COMPANY WE KEEP

2 Corinthians 6:14 KJV. Be ye not unequally yoked together with unbelievers: for what fellowship hath righteousness with unrighteousness? and what communion hath light with darkness?

Paul advised the Corinthians not to be unequally tied or connected to unbelievers. In the agrarian culture of that day, "yoking" was a metaphor they would have understood. When oxen needed to be utilized and controlled, the farmer hitched them to a wagon or plow, then connected them to one another by their necks using a piece of wood called a *yoke*. Once they were yoked together, one ox was not able to move without the other. If one ox was not as strong as the other, they were considered unequally yoked. This would cause them to perform much less efficiently. Paul's use of the metaphor conveyed the idea that believers who are tied with unbelievers will regret it. The believer will be held back in his or her spiritual walk or venture because the unbeliever isn't pulling as strongly, or even in the same direction.

This goes powerfully for our entrepreneurial journeys. Synergy, accountability, and encouragement will be critical for us in our businesses. These are what keep us sharp and motivated (Pr 27:17). For that reason, we must surround ourselves with like-minded individuals who have similar goals, are going in a similar direction, and carry the same spiritual and moral values as we do. To go fast, go alone; but to go far, we need to build teams and networks. Behind every 'self-made' successful entrepreneur is a group of team members, friends, family members, mentors, or investors that had a hand in the success. Networking and building a good team are crucial.

If we end up being "yoked," that is, intricately connected to people who are not headed in the same direction with the same goals, and same spirit, we risk being the ones to lose focus, pulling us away from our own God-given goals and visions. It is simply not possible to walk in two directions at the same time. We will either have to go their way, or they will go ours.

It is ok and even beneficial to spend *some* time with people who have different visions than us, and those who have their own paths. However, we must be careful who we allow ourselves to be "yoked" to, taking inventory of where every relationship in our life and business is leading us, checking in with God, and adjusting accordingly.

Parallel Scriptures:

1 Corinthians 15:33; James 5:16; Ecclesiastes 4:9-10

Dear Lord,

I thank You and praise You for Your kindness in placing all the wonderful people in my life who have helped me. I understand

that everyone You bring around me serves one of Your purposes. Please, Father, open my eyes to see these purposes and reveal to me who I should yoke to. Break every yoke that hinders me in my purpose to fulfill Your calling on my life. Strengthen the bonds I have with those who You've brought in fulfillment of Your purposes to help and bless me to reach my goals. In Jesus' name I pray. Amen.

What is God saying to me? ________________________________

Day 19

HIDDEN GEMS

1 Corinthians 1:27 KJV. But God hath chosen the foolish things of the world to confound the wise; and God hath chosen the weak things of the world to confound the things which are mighty.

In the previous verse, Paul reminded the church at Corinth that not many of those who had joined the church were considered powerful or wise according to human standards. The church was not mostly made up of nobility, the highly educated, or those with high stature and position. It was not Paul's intention to shame the Corinthians by saying this, but to instruct them that God does not require powerful or wise people to accomplish His purposes. As described here, He uses the people who are considered weak and foolish to humble the wise and powerful by showing them how little He thinks of worldly wisdom and worldly power.

Perhaps you sometimes worry that you don't have enough education or wealth to be taken seriously. You wonder why God would choose you to do anything significant. Now you know. God chose you because He saw something in you and could bring Himself glory by blessing you and using you.

In business, we should learn to value what God values, and *who* God values. It is often those who are deemed foolish and impotent by society who can be of the most value. Nuggets of advice and ideas can come from anywhere and anyone. Advice and instruction don't always have to come from a mentor or someone you or society hold in high esteem. Having a strong spirit of discernment is crucial here (Day 9). Be open to ideas and inspiration from everyone during your journey. Be humble about this and you will be amazed where and from whom you will pick up wisdom, even sometimes learning what *not* to do!

Dear Lord,

I have noticed that You have sent many different kinds of people my way to help me and teach me. Thank You, Lord, for each and every one of them. Help me not to discriminate nor to show favoritism, so that I am blind and deaf to the things You are trying to tell me and teach me through these people who You have created. Let me see knowledge when it comes from You, no matter what preconceived notions I have about the messenger You send. Help me to separate the wheat from the chaff, but not to assume I know where the wheat is going to come from. In Jesus' name I pray. Amen.

What is God saying to me? ___

Day 20

COMPARISON KILLS

Exodus 20:17 KJV. Thou shalt not covet thy neighbour's house, thou shalt not covet thy neighbour's wife, nor his manservant, nor his maidservant, nor his ox, nor his ass, nor any thing that is thy neighbour's.

God's final commandment of the Ten Commandments he gave to Moses was, "Thou shalt not covet…" At first, it might not seem that big of a deal that we could want what someone else has, as long as we don't steal it. But, theft, murder, and other commandments that are broken often start with this one. At the very least, coveting anything that belongs to our neighbor shows God that we are not content with what we currently have.

On our entrepreneurship journeys we will see many others traveling at different paces on their own paths. Some will be ahead of us where we'd like to someday be. Benchmarking, or using these as inspiration, is fine. It's a great practice. However, issues arise when we begin to strongly desire and yearn for what others have. This is dangerous, not only because it undermines our own path, but also because we very seldom know what these companies have done to get where they are. Many times, we will learn that these companies have participated in illegal actions, or unethical ones to establish their rise. Without these actions, some companies may not have stood the test of time, or grown so large. These practices are not something we should want to emulate.

Other companies may have simply faced grueling challenges along the way that we'll never know about. Did the cost of their success come at a price higher than we are willing to pay? It is worth asking the question because our business is not the only element of a well-lived life for the glory of God. Did their success come at the cost of their marriage, or their relationship with their children? Did they forego church participation in order to be workaholics? A good business model will allow for our faithfulness in every area God has assigned to us. We often only see the successes of finished brands and miss all the struggles that were endured to get there. Comparison kills. We must learn to appreciate our own journeys and congratulate others for their success without coveting what they have. God has a unique plan for each of us. We must spend the majority of our time looking at Him, and not at the success of others.

Dear Lord,

I am so grateful for this place that I am in at this very moment that You have ordained for me. I know that it is exactly where I should be, and I thank You that You have ordained it. I pray that You would help me to appreciate my own journey, and my own

path straight ahead, and not to look to the left or the right at the journeys of others. I know that this would be a trap and would end badly. You have blessed me with the only journey that is mine. You ordained it before I was born, and it was written in eternity. Thank You, Lord. In Jesus' name I pray. Amen.

What is God saying to me?

Day 21

REMAIN TEACHABLE

Matthew 18:3-4 KJV. 3 And said, "Verily I say unto you, Except ye be converted, and become as little children, ye shall not enter into the kingdom of heaven. 4 Whosoever therefore shall humble himself as this little child, the same is greatest in the kingdom of heaven."

The disciples asked Jesus who is the greatest in the kingdom of heaven. Isn't that a strange question? Why else would you ask that unless you were hoping it would be yourself? Jesus burst everyone's bubble by bringing forth a child, and He explained that a little child is the greatest in the kingdom of heaven. He explained that someone who takes the lowest and humblest position is the greatest in His kingdom.

The Bible, from front to back, teaches that the greatest virtue aside from Love is humility. Jesus warns us not to have a prideful attitude, and Paul tells us to boast only on the cross of Jesus Christ (Gal 6:14 NIV). While children can have their challenges and must be taught many things, they typically display some good natural qualities. They usually respect authority, are trusting, teachable, and optimistic, believing they can accomplish anything they set their minds to. Society bears the responsibility for killing the dreams and imaginations of children. Jesus would have us look to them for a fresh and innocent attitude about life and a great faith in God, unmarred by the cynicism that sets in after some time in this life. Jesus would have us remain humble and teachable.

As entrepreneurs, it is important that we have not only the humility of children as outlined by this Scripture, but a spirit that trusts God completely. Teachability is an extremely important quality for us, and let's not forget when we had the great imagination of a child. Arrogance and pride often lead to ignorance. We need humility and teachability so that we can stand on the shoulders of giants and go forward. When we face setbacks, great or small, we need humility. Perhaps we will face a day when what we have spent years building comes to nothing. Will we have the humility and imagination to pick up our tools and begin building again, humbler and wiser than before? There are no guarantees as entrepreneurs that our journeys will be easy on the ego. Humility will see us through to the end.

Dear Lord,

Thank You for all the lessons You have taught me and will teach me in the future. Everything You have taught me is for my good, and I would not want to have missed any of it. Bless me as I grow to remain humble and teachable so that I will not miss a single lesson from You going forward. All that You teach me is valuable, whether it is a big lesson or a small one. Mold my attitude. I want to be humble, receptive, and to delight in correction when it

is necessary, because I know that is how You will grow me into who and what You want me to be. In Jesus' name I pray. Amen.

What is God saying to me?

Day 22

STRATEGIC PLACEMENT OF YOUR LIFE'S INFLUENCERS

1 Corinthians 3:7-11 KJV. 7 So then neither is he that planteth any thing, neither he that watereth; but God that giveth the increase. 8 Now he that planteth and he that watereth are one: and every man shall receive his own reward according to his own labour. 9 For we are labourers together with God: ye are God's husbandry, ye are God's building. 10 According to the grace of God which is given unto me, as a wise masterbuilder, I have laid the foundation, and another buildeth thereon. But let every man take heed how he buildeth thereupon. 11 For other foundation can no man lay than that is laid, which is Jesus Christ.

Paul said that one person waters after another person plants, and salvation is the ultimate goal. His point was that no one can do God's mission alone. He intended for His church to function as a body, with everyone having a part to play (1 Cor 12:12-27). Paul laid a foundation as a masterbuilder, but *each man* will have to build on that foundation in the way that God has planned for them to build on the foundation of Jesus Christ. In this way, each man or woman will be rewarded for his or her own faithfulness and God's purposes of salvation will be achieved.

As entrepreneurs, our businesses will function in the same way. A myriad of people will plant seeds in your life. You will plant seeds, knowingly or unknowingly, in the lives of others. But ultimately, it is God who orders our steps and the steps of others to get those seeds planted (Day 29). God is responsible for all the increase. No one person can claim credit for anyone else's success, only God. The culmination of all the seeds planted was ordained by God before the foundation of the world. As 1 Corinthians 3:11 suggests, everyone has a purpose as a worker and a purpose in the lives of others. Both of these are ordained by God.

We are all spiritual houses. In verses 10 and 11, God creates the foundation, and everyone we come into contact with are laborers, *hired* by God to help build our houses. We must take wisdom and inspiration from others. We must listen and reflect on what each person we have encountered has taught us (Day 9) (Day 19). People have various roles in our lives. Some will play more crucial roles than others, but we can learn something from every person we encounter on our journey (Day 19). Some things we will take with us on our journey, others we will leave behind, learning rather what *not* to do by their example. Everyone has their own perspective. Every single person you meet presents an opportunity to learn, serving as a builder on the foundation that God has begun. Learn and receive the valuable nuggets from them all.

Dear Lord,

Thank You for everyone who You have used to plant seeds in my life. Thank You for using me to plant seeds in the lives of others. It has been a blessing and privilege to be used by You. Lord, help me to understand and know that no human is responsible for my success, and that no human ever will be responsible for my success. I confess, Lord, that You and You alone, according to my obedience, are the One responsible for my success, and I humbly thank You, Lord. In Jesus' name I pray. Amen.

What is God saying to me?

Day 23

ELEVATOR TESTIMONY

1 Peter 3:15 KJV. But sanctify the Lord God in your hearts: and be ready always to give an answer to every man that asketh you a reason of the hope that is in you with meekness and fear.

It is so important that we as Christians are always able to explain to curious people why we chose to walk with Jesus Christ. This might be the only time this person will hear the Good News about Jesus. God may have ordained this as their chance to get what you have and be led to Christ, starting their walk with Him. Often, we will be given very little time to explain why we love Jesus and choose to follow Him.

In business, this is called our *elevator speech.* Do you have one? If you've never heard of an elevator speech, just imagine you are on an elevator with another person and you need to make your best sales pitch in the short time they are riding it with you. Soon, they will arrive at their floor, and you have lost your chance. Can you get all the key points into succinct and gripping statements? We need to be able to say what our company provides with precision and confidence. Practice this with your friends and family.

So, what about your faith *elevator speech [testimony]*? You need one because the Bible says to always be ready. Who is Jesus to you, and what has He done for the world, including you specifically? Why did He come? What was wrong with the world that needed fixing? What's going to happen next? Think about all those things and be ready.

Peter also says to, "sanctify the Lord God in your hearts." Or as the NIV puts it, "But in your hearts revere Christ as LORD." Start there. Do you revere Christ in your heart? Cultivate this every day. If He is not revered in your heart, you will miss opportunities to share Jesus, because you'll simply forget. Would you forget to share about your business when you meet a potential customer? No, because you have set aside your business in your heart as important.

Peter also says, "But do this with gentleness and respect" (NIV). It is not just what you say, but how you say it. Proverbs 18:19 says, "A brother offended is harder to be won than a strong city: and their contentions are like the bars of a castle." If you are pushy or offensive, you will not display the nature and character of Christ, and you will forfeit the privilege of sharing your testimony. The same goes with your business pitch. Who you are, especially when it comes to how you treat people, will open doors for you to share about your business, or it will close doors.

This chapter should not be confused as saying that you should share Jesus like a salesman. This should be real and authentic. You do it because you have sanctified Jesus in your heart, and it matters to you what happens to people. If you cannot share your business in the same way, then you don't really believe in your idea. We should not expect that our business idea has the same weight as the Gospel. It doesn't. But if we don't truly believe in it, then we should keep looking for a product that we do believe in. Ideally, God will grant you the ability and opportunity to do both for the glory of God: sharing your business, and more importantly, sharing Christ. Hopefully, you will have more than an elevator ride to do so, but you must be prepared for the opportunities when they come, no matter how limited on time.

Parallel Scripture:

Matthew 24:44

Dear Lord,

Thank You for the opportunities that You have given me, and will give me to spread my messages. Grant me the courage to spread the good news about my business, and even more importantly, the good news about Your Son, Jesus Christ, and His death and resurrection for the redemption of our sins. I pray that You will make my elevator speech become second nature to me, and that You will place ample opportunities in my path to share these messages with those who are able to benefit from them and take them further. In Jesus' name I pray. Amen.

What is God saying to me? ______________________________

Day 24

YOUR NEW PERSPECTIVE ON HARD WORK

Colossians 3:23 KJV. And whatsoever ye do, do it heartily, as to the Lord, and not unto men;

The context for this verse is the instruction to bond servants that they should obey their masters not only when they are being watched, appearing to do good, but obeying even when no one is watching and with complete sincerity. In this way, we are to work for God, rather than men. God is always watching, so it is not hard to obey as though we are working for Christ. To work "heartily" means that we should do the work completely, fully, and with all our whole heart. If, by faith, we could truly work this way and with this mindset, just imagine the effort we would put in and the results we would get!

If we have the mindset that everything we do is for our God, then we will not cut corners or turn in half efforts, giving less than our very best. We won't turn in half-completed assignments. Maybe some of us have day jobs that we dislike. Maybe there are aspects of our business that we don't find enjoyable, but they are necessary to do if we are going to be successful. God would have us see these as an opportunity to serve Him through serving others. Regardless of what other people around are doing, cutting corners, taking extra-long breaks, giving less than their best, we are called to be different, working diligently and *heartily* at whatever we are tasked with.

Many of us became entrepreneurs because we wanted to be our own boss, but the fact is, our main boss is in heaven. The job description He has given us is *faithful.* The way we do one thing is the way we do all things. This may take some work, but we need to build up work ethic as one of our main habits so that we can always put forth our very best effort for God's glory. As we build our businesses, we need to learn to take on every task as if it were being done directly for an audience of One, our Father in heaven. In this way, we bring honor to the One who created us, and we are guaranteed to see improvements in the quality of our work.

Dear Lord,

I confess that I sometimes don't want to work as hard as I should. Yet, thank You for showing me that hard work is needed in order to fulfill the goals You have given me. Thank You that You have given me the discipline and desire to do that hard work. Help me to learn how to approach this work knowing that it is for You. Show me how to give my very best effort to every task, realizing that it is for Your glory that I accomplish it. In Jesus' name I pray. Amen.

What is God saying to me?

Day 25

SPIRITUAL DISCIPLINE

Hebrews 12:11-12 KJV. 11 Now no chastening for the present seemeth to be joyous, but grievous: nevertheless afterward it yieldeth the peaceable fruit of righteousness unto them which are exercised thereby. 12 Wherefore lift up the hands which hang down, and the feeble knees.

The first step to freedom is *discipline.* Without discipline we are prisoners of our impulses and indulgences. Imagine: on one side of a chasm are our goals written out. On the other side is the accomplishment of all those goals. There is a bridge that connects the two sides and that is *discipline.* The vehicle that drives across the bridge is hard work (Day 24). Without discipline we will be haunted by our aspirations, always wanting to fulfill them, but never able to accomplish them. Discipline makes the time we spend on a task more effective and intense. We simply must take the time to learn great habits, cutting bad habits, stepping out of our comfort zones, and removing ourselves from unproductive groups. All of these crucial steps take great discipline. As Hebrews 12:11-12 suggests, doing these things involves enduring a certain amount of pain.

Spiritually, when we are disciplined by God, we gain spiritual success, or righteousness and peace. This is His promise to us if we allow ourselves to be trained by His discipline. In a similar way, we will reap success and peace in our businesses if we stick to it and allow ourselves to be shaped by the disciplines of productivity.

God's discipline for us is according to His purposes and plans. It is for fighting against [crucifying] our flesh (Gal 5:24). We are creatures of habit. Any discipline, whether self-inflicted or given by an authority, is a war against your innate drive to continue a course of habit. It is extremely important for us to take every thought captive (2 Cor 10:5), for the war of discipline is first won in our mind (Ro 12:2).

In business, we might need discipline to methodically reinvest our profits back into the company, rather than squandering them on personal pleasures. It might mean scheduling daily time to work on a particular business goal. Being disciplined will help us to create order and eliminate the confusion that causes so much inefficiency. Habits of good discipline should be established as early as possible in our business. We won't always *feel* motivated to complete tasks and do the hard but right things. Discipline is what will allow us to do them anyway.

God is the God of order and not confusion (1 Cor 14:33). Plan. Routine. Schedule. In verse 12, it says to strengthen our feeble arms and weak knees. God doesn't tell us to shy away from discipline, but for us to get stronger and endure the process.

Parallel Scriptures:

Proverbs 25:28; Romans 8:6

Dear Lord,

I have seen that tough times produce good things in me, like self-discipline. Thank You for the fact that no tough times are wasted, but all of them are full of purpose. Help me not to shy away from the moments that come which seem to go against the habits I have created. In the discomfort that You have ordained, allow me to find perfect peace, because I know that in these very times You are building me, growing me, and producing self-discipline in me. Thank You in advance for what I will be in many years down the road if I have the grace to accept Your lessons. In Jesus' name I pray. Amen.

What is God saying to me? ______________________________

Day 26

JUMP

Matthew 14:22-34 KJV.

Peter, an experienced fisherman and boatman, was on rough waters with the other disciples, their craft being tossed about. Suddenly, a figure approached, skimming the top of the water like a ghost of some sort. They were terrified. The entity came close and insisted that it was Jesus coming to them. Peter stepped up to challenge the entity and said that if it was Jesus, then it should allow Peter to walk to him on the top of the water. Peter took a leap of faith from the boat and actually began to walk toward Jesus on the water! But then, Peter's mind redirected from Christ to the wind and the waves. He began to doubt, and then he began to sink, looking back to Jesus with terror in his eyes. His fear overcame him.

Similarly, the "conditions" before and after we begin our entrepreneurial journey will not always look the most favorable before we feel we must take the leap of faith into starting our business. Peter was surrounded by others who doubted, and who would never have jumped in that water. Likewise, we are surrounded by doubters all throughout our own entrepreneurial journeys. They may doubt your abilities, your ideas, or your toughness. The boat represented safety and comfort for Peter. It was his only protection from the harsh conditions. But the thing he desired most was just *outside* the boat, right in the *midst* of the uncertainty and danger.

Entrepreneurship is neither comfortable nor safe. The thing we desire most, success in our venture, lies outside the safety zone, shrouded in harsh and uncertain conditions. Peter knew the windy and tumultuous conditions of the water before he jumped, but his focus was on his goal, Jesus. We should be aware, but not afraid of conditions in our own journeys. We should be aware enough to deal with them realistically, but not crippled or paralyzed by them so that we don't start. We must keep our own eyes fixed on Jesus *and* the vision He has given us. It takes a faithful person like Peter to jump into a business idea. We should not allow the fearful others in our *boats*, or the harsh conditions outside to keep us from jumping. By focusing on Jesus and our mission, we will prevail.

Dear Lord,

Thank You for inviting me to jump into this business opportunity. I pray that I could be aware of the noise around me, but not focused on it. Rather, help me to keep my eyes on You and on the goals You have put before me. Give me the courage to wisely jump out of the current boat of safety that I am in, and into this new idea, even when it looks like wind and waves. Allow me to use any noise around me as motivation to continue the straight path ahead that You have made for me. In Jesus' name I pray. Amen.

What is God saying to me? ______________________________

Day 27

EVERYTHING WILL WORK IN YOUR FAVOR

Romans 8:28 KJV. And we know that all things work together for good to them that love God, to them who are the called according to his purpose.

Through the lens of hindsight, it is always easier to connect the dots that made up our success. What we must do is trust that the dots will connect moving forward. The good news for us according to this Scripture is that God will connect the dots for us. Even if your first, second, or third business ideas do not prosper, you are on an entrepreneurial journey and are gaining valuable skills and wisdom along the way. Don't underestimate the interpersonal skills, the intrapersonal skills, the financial skills, the administrative, marketing, and other skills you have been gaining along the way. Take everything as a lesson learned and keep going. Find in every setback an opportunity for growth towards becoming the best entrepreneur you can be. There are lessons in every loss. Learn to see them. Learn to find the redirections in every failure. Every roadblock is steering you closer to the correct path.

This is exciting. If we can learn this, we will never look at failure in the same way again. The failure to see life this way is the number one reason why people fail at business. They quit. They quit because they don't understand the purpose of failures. It would be very nice if our first idea was a homerun, and we never had to think or work again. But, then again, would it be that nice? The entrepreneurial journey is just that, a journey. The journey, with all its setbacks and winding roads, is part of the greatness of the venture. We are called to produce. We are called to produce *a certain product,* and this verse promises that we are called "according to His purpose." And this means that absolutely everything that happens as we faithfully walk this path "work[s] together for good to them that love God, to them who are called according to his purpose."

God will not put anything on us that we cannot bear, or that is not good for us. He will not even give us otherwise *good* things if it is not what we need to live according to His good purpose for us, and if it will harm us. Trust Him and walk His path for you. Thank Him not only for the successes, but the failures and closed doors that make the right path clearer. The dots *will* connect in the end. Trust Him.

Parallel Scripture:

James 1:2-3

Dear Lord,

Thank You for my specific business journey. Thank You for each and every success, and even every setback. I love You, and confess that I am one of those called according to Your purposes. Thank You for Your grace and mercy in my life. I have great assurance that every outcome of this journey that I am on will work out for my ultimate good. This assurance gives me a peace that surpasses all understanding. In Jesus' name I pray. Amen.

What is God saying to me? ______________________________

Day 28

MOTIVES FOR STARTING/REMEMBER WHY YOU STARTED

Galatians 1:10 NIV. Am I now trying to win the approval of human beings, or of God? Or am I trying to please people? If I were still trying to please people, I would not be a servant of Christ.

We must always remember why we started the entrepreneurial journey, because it is easy to forget. While we are chasing our goals, changing our brand as customers and mentors give feedback, or following market trends, we must remember our niche, and we must remember what motivated us to start in the first place. This is what will help us to stay the course and weather the storms on this journey.

In our day currently, the title of *entrepreneur* has become an overinflated, glorified moniker that many are eager to bear. At one time, having a solid nine to five job with a major company was the thing to boast about. At that time, saying you were starting your own business was like saying you were unemployed, having nothing solid for yourself. Reflect and introspect on this: are you in business to *show off* or *impress* other people? Or rather, are you in business to *help* other people? Those companies that are truly successful are the ones who exist to make others' lives better. We must ask ourselves this question: Whose life will be made better by the success of our venture? Our purpose is wrapped up in serving others with our gifts (Day 1). If we speak and work our companies into existence, and they become large and successful, we must not then get caught up in showing off. That would prove that the whole reason for doing this was to impress other people.

Paul had it right. We are not to pursue our calling in order to impress others. That is an empty goal. Jesus said we would lose our reward if we practiced our righteousness to be seen by others (Mt 6). Lay down the desire to impress man. Do what you do for the sake of God. He has already approved of you in His Son, Jesus Christ. Now, you can live for Him with all your might, bringing glory to Him as His image-bearing producer of what work He has given you to do. But, if you are still trying to impress man, He will not bless it. Lay that down and live for Him.

Parallel Scripture:

James 4:3 NIV

Dear Lord,

Thank You for allowing me to see myself rightly so that I can see when there are impure or selfish motives throughout my journey. I pray that You will help me to correct these false intentions.

Also, Lord, help me to remember that this endeavor is not for me, but for the people who I can serve and whose lives can be improved, especially those who could be pointed to You by my work. I pray that You will continue to connect me with those You have planned for me to impact with my work and with my testimony. In Jesus' name I pray. Amen.

What is God saying to me? ___

Day 29

THE IMPORTANCE OF ORDAINED STEPS

Proverbs 16:9 KJV. A man's heart deviseth his way: but the Lord directeth his steps.

Proverbs 16:3 KJV. Commit thy works unto the Lord, and thy thoughts shall be established.

All of our actions begin as thoughts in our hearts (Pr 23:7; Mt 15:18; Mt 12:34; Lk 6:45). God's promise to us is that if we first commit our work to Him, He will establish our thoughts (Pr 16:3). If God only has plans to prosper us and not harm us (Jer 29:11), then these established thoughts are exactly what we need for our ventures to succeed.

The absolutely crucial step is to commit our work to Him. Are you living for God and for His purposes and glory? Have you told Him that? Have you told Him that He can have you and your business, and do whatever He wants to do with it? If so, did you really mean it? That is step one and the most critical.

Step two is then to flesh out the thoughts He is giving us. These things should happen daily as we recommit to our work to Him. Daily, we should pray, and then write out our thoughts, looking back at the previous thoughts and directions He has given us.

Step three is to then walk according to His plan for us, according to the thoughts. The direction we are heading will always be much more important than the speed we are going. There are many people who are traveling very quickly in the opposite direction of their God-given vision. It is of the utmost importance to have our steps ordered by God. He has a plan, but we need to follow it if we have committed our work to Him. When we chase God's plan and no longer chase the achievements, the achievements start chasing us.

Parallel Scriptures:

Psalm 37:23; Jeremiah 10:23

Dear Lord,

You have promised that if I commit my venture to You, You will establish all my steps. I believe this. I pray that You will give me the grace to trust in You more and more so that I will genuinely, freely, and readily commit my plans to You. I confess that in my flesh I can forget to do this. Lord, direct my steps and order my thoughts as I give You full control of my life and business. I do not want any outcome that does not please You and work according to Your plans to use me to bring glory to Your name for the good of the world. In Jesus' name I pray. Amen.

What is God saying to me? ______________________________

Day 30

QUIET TIME

Luke 22:41 KJV. And he was withdrawn from them about a stone's cast, and kneeled down, and prayed,

Everyone wanted to be around Jesus all the time. He drew mighty crowds and great multitudes of people who clamored to touch Him and hear from Him. This was exactly why He came: to draw men and women to Himself. Even so, it is truly amazing to see how often the Bible tells us that He withdrew Himself, sending people away.

Resting in the presence of God is just as important, if not more important than our work. When Jesus was facing His greatest task, that of being rejected, mocked, beaten, falsely tried in a kangaroo court, hung on a cross, and filled with the sins of the world, He was, understandably, anxious. He had never before experienced the broken fellowship with His Father in heaven. How would He endure this, let alone the mental and physical anguish? This was His Father's will for Him, but He, perfect as He was, did not feel ready for it. Jesus had to get away to get His mind right.

None of us are facing what Jesus faced, but we too need to get away from people regularly with God, so that we can refocus on our task with Him and get our minds right. Jesus was God. The fact that He needed to do this should give us no doubt that we need to do it. Before you have anything big to do, you should get away with God (Lk 4:1-2). Just after you have done something big, go get with Him and recharge (Mk 6:30-32). Every morning when you wake, get with Him. We do not know what each day will bring, but God can make us ready if we will go and be with Him. If we want our steps to be ordained by Him (Day 29), then we must go and be with Him.

Jesus often withdrew himself to go to the wilderness and pray (Lk 5:16 NIV). However, we saw in Luke 22:41 that Jesus did not have to go far, but He had to go. Even if it is only a "stone's cast" away, withdraw yourself and hear from God. During our entrepreneurial journeys, there will be plenty of times when we need space from family and friends to work on our craft as we are led by God. He is always trying to talk to us, giving us inspiration and direction. We only need enough silence to hear Him.

Parallel Scriptures:

Luke 5:16, Mark 1:35, Matthew 14:23

Dear Lord,

I see that it is extremely important to spend quality time with You. Thank You for teaching me that. I see that even Your Son, Jesus Christ, who was in very nature, God, needed consistent quality time alone with You each day. I pray that You would help me to learn to withdraw myself physically and mentally to be with

You in solitude, so that I can learn to recharge in prayer for everything You have designed for me to do. I pray that I would do it early and often every day. Thank You in advance for the grace to obey You in this. In Jesus' name I pray. Amen.

What is God saying to me?

Day 31

GIVING & FIRST FRUITS

Matthew 25:35-40 KJV.

God put a special meaning behind giving and placed special power on what we give. Giving is a reciprocal principle in both the natural and spiritual realms - sowing and reaping. God calls us to be like streams, flowing with compassion, giving generously to others. He doesn't call us to be reservoirs, selfishly holding our gifts and resources to ourselves. When we give, volunteer our time, and accommodate those in need (the least of these as God calls them), God likens it to if we are doing those things for Him and will bless us for it (Mt 25:35-40).

Many successful people have made it a habit to give. They've come to understand the principle of giving that givers are always re-warded. When we give, though, we must have the correct intentions and motives for giving, giving out of love, joy, and compassion, never seeking anything from those we give to.

When we tithe on our harvests to God to build His Kingdom, He promises that He will protect our ventures (Mal 3:11-12). Giving to God and His Kingdom to see a return on what we give is the one thing in the Bible that God permits us to test Him in. In Malachi 3:10-12, God promises us that when we tithe to God (especially sacrificially, when it costs us to do so) He will bless us with more than we had and protect our endeavors. Tithes to God do not always have to be monetary. One can tithe on his or her time or energy to build God's Kingdom as an offering. God will not call us to do something that He himself, Jesus, or any illustrated biblical example has not already done. As the ultimate example of giving, God gave His only son, Jesus, to the world to be sacrificed for our sins.

As entrepreneurs, we often start with very little, scraping up our resources to start our ventures. If we can learn to even find ways to give our resources selflessly to others in need when we have little, God will bless the little we have. Giving when we have little will condition us to learn how to give more when we receive more. Discernment is key here so that we give and sow wisely and in fertile ground that is for Kingdom building (Day 9). If we become accustomed to setting aside part of our harvest for tithes to God's Kingdom, it will be easy for us to set aside parts of our harvest in business for Uncle Sam, as we were already conditioned to do so.

Dear Lord,

I ask that You renew my mind and remove any selfishness that may come in the way of me giving. I ask that You show me what I

have now that I am able to give. Please bless my endeavors, so that I will be able to give even more. In Jesus' name I pray. Amen.

What is God saying to me? ______________________________

ABOUT THE AUTHOR

Ronald Callender Jr. graduated from the University of Maryland, Baltimore County in 2013 with a Bachelor's degree in Business Technology Administration. He then graduated from Grenoble Graduate School of Business in Grenoble, France in 2016 with a Master's Degree in International Business. At twenty-three years of age, while living in France and completing his graduate studies, he began his first official business venture as he founded the fashion brand, Ainsley & Troupe. With features in GQ Magazine, Glamour Magazine, ABC7 News, and other major news and television platforms, Ainsley & Troupe is a major up and coming men's fashion brand at the time of this writing. Ainsley & Troupe has styled and outfitted celebrity clients and clients who work in the West Wing of the White House.

Ronald has been involved in entrepreneurship all his life. His mother, Toni Callender, an ordained minister, helped him strengthen his faith from an early age, encouraging him that he could do whatever he wanted in life with God at the helm. Ronald grew up in an environment that cultivated his mind for business, having parents who encouraged him to enter fashion entrepreneurship at seven years of age with his older brother, Jamal, when the two started their own fashion company. From there, Ronald spent time pursuing many entrepreneurial endeavors as a young man, including selling candy in elementary school, and hand-painting and airbrushing custom sneakers and t-shirts for friends and classmates in high school. While Ronald had plans and hopes to do many things growing up, from working on Wall Street, to becoming a professional chef, psychologist, professional athlete, or fashion designer, it was during his early adult life that he began to truly seek what his purpose in life was. During his self-discovery, God revealed that two of his great callings in life would be fashion and teaching. One of the ways God revealed these to Ronald was through learning the meaning of his names.

Ronald - advisor, counselor: Ronald regularly coaches and teaches others through mediums such as this book;

Ainsley - to live in solitude alongside nature: nature is the primary design inspiration for his fashion brand, Ainsley & Troupe;

Callender - an early English occupational name for a person who finished freshly woven cloth by passing it between heavy rollers to compress the weave: he uses his gifts for designing, creating, and styling clothing through Ainsley & Troupe.

This devotional is a culmination of spiritual lessons Ronald has learned throughout his lifelong walk with Jesus Christ, combined with his business knowledge gained as an entrepreneur and business coach, in corporate America, and from his formal business education.

ACKNOWLEDGEMENTS

This work would not have been possible without key players God placed in my life.

My parents, Toni and Ronald Callender Sr., taught me the perfect blend of discipline and *crazy* faith. Mom, thank you for raising me as a God-fearing man, encouraging me to develop my own relationship with Him. Thank you for giving me the crazy faith to believe I can do anything I set my mind towards at a young age. Pops, thank you for teaching me how to take my crazy faith and look at things practically, and to break everything down into actionable items. Thank you for passing down the level of discipline you gained from your service in the U.S. Army. Everything you both taught me growing up continued to make more and more sense as I entered adulthood.

My brothers in Christ, Gerald Collins, Craig Hines, Carrington Dennis, and Owen Hart, thank you for your daily fellowship and keeping me focused to keep the main thing (God) the main thing. Friends and loved ones, thank you for all your support in my personal and business endeavors. Sohrab Malik, Armani Mason-Callaway, Eric Reynolds, Ijeoma Agbaraji, John Barr, Heaven Manley, Mike Martin, Daryl Omire-Mayor, and Phillip Hickman, I sincerely thank you all for being obedient to God in your respective ways to help me pursue my dreams.

1 COR 3:7-8
PRO 14:23